MAKE
HASTE
—*My*—
BELOVED

FRANCES J. ROBERTS

BARBOUR
PUBLISHING

ISBN 1-59310-290-9

Library of Congress Cataloging-in-Publication Data

Roberts, Frances J.
    Make haste my beloved / Frances J. Roberts.
        p. cm.
 ISBN 1-59310-290-9 (pbk.)
 1. Devotional literature. 2. Christian Literature. I. Title.

 BV4801.R66 2004
 242—dc22

                    2004004894

Published by Barbour Publishing, Inc., P.O. Box 719, Uhrichsville, Ohio
44683, www.barbourbooks.com

Our mission is to publish and distribute inspirational products offering exceptional value and biblical encouragement to the masses.

Member of the
Evangelical Christian
Publishers Association

Printed in the United States of America.
5 4 3 2 1

MAKE HASTE
HASTE
—*My*—
BELOVED

Contents

INTRODUCTION

*Make haste, my beloved,
and be thou like to a roe or to a young hart
upon the mountains of spices.*

SONG OF SOLOMON 8:14

It is the call of the bride to the bridegroom as she cries, "Make haste, my beloved." It is indeed heartening to know that it is HE who makes the haste! We are forever aware of how painfully slow we travel on our journey toward sainthood. The desire is in our hearts to know and walk with God; but the detaining influences within our own hearts and in the world about us contrive to hold us back. And so we cry to Him, our heavenly bridegroom, "Make haste, and *come to me!*"

Let us be encouraged when we realize how slowly we move toward Him, for in response to our desire He is able to move swiftly toward us! There is nothing to prevent Him from coming to us in the place of devotion except our failure to seek His companionship. We may experience the sweetness of communion with Him to the degree that we wait upon Him in prayer and adoration.

In verse 17 of the second chapter of the Song of Solomon we read "Turn, my beloved, and be thou like a roe or a young hart upon the mountains of *Bether.*" The meaning of Bether is *separation*. This was at a point where the bride was seeking the bridegroom but had not found Him. Now, in chapter 8:14, Bether is not mentioned, but rather, the mountains of spices. The Church has passed through seasons of lapse and separation when intimate fellowship with her Lord was all but lost. Let it be the sincere intention of His bride in these days of nearness to His coming, that she may meet Him in the mountains of spices —in the sweet fragrance of a renewed first love and the white fire of true devotion.

Yes, *Make Haste, My Beloved!*

THE SECRET *of the* UNIVERSE

Tell Me, My child, your deepest longings, and in all your searching, come to Me. I am always found of them who seek and ready to help the soul in need. It is your need that draws Me to your aid. You feel a need and cannot identify it. I know that in My presence it will be dissolved, because I know it is My love for which you yearn. "In My presence is fulness of joy"; therefore I know that as you drink of the fresh waters of My Spirit you shall be refreshed.

I do not tell you a new thing. I only say again what I have said so many times before: Come unto Me. You shall find rest for your soul, relief from your burdens, and quietness of spirit.

There is no turmoil in the soul that rests in My bosom. There is turmoil in the world, but you are not of the world, My little one. You belong to Me. You are Mine, and I have called you apart into a walk of faith, of holiness, of communion with Me. Never go back to the beggarly elements in quest of comfort. Your spirit knows the Fountain of Life. Your heart knows but one love. . .the love of Christ; and from that one love comes the grace to embrace all creatures with understanding and compassion.

It is in the act of worship the soul is sanctified. *"Thou shalt love the Lord thy God with all thy heart, and Him only shalt thou serve."* To love and worship any other is the path of destruction. I will keep you from false worship as you give yourself to Me in submission to Truth. Truth is revealed in My Word. Make it your daily meat and drink. Bind it to the doorposts of your mind. Store it in your heart. Write it upon your walls. Speak it to your children. Pursue Truth, and forsake it not. It is My life poured out for you through the eternal revelation of the Holy Scriptures. It is infallible. It has power to bind evil and to release good. It is the storehouse of wisdom and the source of life. *It is the secret of the universe,* and you shall not add to nor take from.

Through My Word I have shared with you the fullness of My life. As My Spirit breathes upon its truths, you shall discover riches and depths beyond your present understanding. Look not elsewhere for added revelation. Truth is revealed not according to content but according to receptivity. Suddenly a truth becomes real to you. The truth is not new: *Its revelation to you is new.* My Word is ever, and will continue to be, the unfailing source of spiritual life and understanding. Man in his pride seeks elsewhere for knowledge, looking to other men for enlightenment. He drinks from other cups when he ought to come to the fountain. He looks to the creature when he ought to worship the Creator.

You know, My child, the source of all your good. Seek Me with your whole heart. I will bless and reward in ways beyond your expectation.

THE PROPHET'S TONGUE

No prophet of Mine is worthy of the name who brings reproach upon Zion by a careless tongue. He who speaks My words at any time must guard his lips at ALL times. He is an unworthy mouthpiece who delivers My message in one breath and denies Me in a selfish moment by words that offend My Spirit.

"Let your speech be alway with grace, seasoned with salt" (Colossians 4:6).

INNER RESOURCES

Never allow circumstances to frighten you, My child. You are not defeated by outer circumstances, but by inner weakness. Whenever you are challenged, look not at the magnitude of the problem, but examine your inner resources. Out of the abundance of My Spirit within you shall come the necessary strength to meet the demand; nothing shall confront you that is greater than My grace.

It is easy to walk in the Spirit, because to do so implies the flow of My life through your heart, your mind, your actions, and your speech. It is the life of Christ made manifest. It is the new creature displacing the old. It is the kingdom of God evidenced where once reigned the kingdom of self. It is love supplanting hatred, and righteousness triumphing over evil. It is hope, joy, and peace. It is kindness, tolerance, and understanding.

To move in love is to move in power, and the deeper the love, the more effective its action upon the total personality.

Out of joy comes health and strength; for the life of the Spirit is sustained within the human heart by faith, and faith is an inseparable companion to joy. It is joy that lifts the soul above the clouds of affliction into the sunshine of God's abiding love. It is joy that turns despair to confidence and sweetens the bitter waters of sorrow.

To rejoice is to cease to doubt. The joyous spirit is in harmony with the heart of God who knows no discouragement nor countenances evil. Joy does not see the darkness of the night but the brilliance of the stars. Better a cup full of joy than a vault filled with riches. All the wealth of the world cannot buy joy, and all the powers of hell cannot take it from the one who has made it his possession.

And how is it to be possessed? It is by the abandonment of selfish demands and the acceptance of the Father's will. It is by forming the daily habit of seeking to please Him in all things. . .not as a burdensome duty, but as an outer expression of an inner love. It is the heart of the cross fulfilled in human experience. Stated in most simple terms, it is to love God; for no man who loves Him can long be sad. He is a fountain of joy. He is the epitome of consolation. "Come unto Me, all who struggle and strive, for I will be your comfort." *("Come unto me, all ye who labour and are heavy laden and I will give you rest.")* To rest is to rejoice, and to rejoice is to be at rest.

He who does not know how to rest and rejoice, let him employ his leisure thoughts in blessing all who come to mind, and in so doing, he shall find blessings showered upon his own head, and he shall rejoice because his cup is filled. Never pray only that God will fill your own cup: Pray rather that He will fill the cup of another, for it is written that he who gives shall also receive. It is one of the inescapable laws of the Spirit. It is the passport to delight. *"Delight thyself in the Lord, and he shall give thee the desires of thine heart."* Can one be sad who has received from the Father the desires of his heart (Psalm 37:4)?

HEAVEN IS YOUR PORTION

You are faltering on the threshold of understanding, My child. Only the courageous discover My riches. Faintheart will content himself with what his eye beholds. The Spirit in you is wiser and will gladly fling aside all material blessings to lay hold on eternal life. The Spirit is not enticed by the glitter of gold nor tempted to desert heavenly vision in favor of temporal blessings.

It is My love that will reveal to you the path of true life. Your own heart will look for outer comfort. The only true comfort, My child, is the comfort of My Spirit, and I am within you, ministering continually in behalf of your eternal spirit, as the priest who stood daily in the temple offering prayers and sacrifices. This I am doing for you. The greatest joy you can know is yours as your own spirit joins with My Spirit in this holy worship. You may be in a cathedral or in a tent. . .alone or in the company of others: My Spirit continues to worship within the temple of your heart.

The moment you join Me in true, conscious *worship*, you experience joy and release. You are blessed and re-freshed. All that salvation brings you is activated in that moment. Prayer is answered, sin is forgiven, fear is banished, peace is restored, and the soul is at rest with its own self and with its Maker.

Yes, heaven is your portion as you WORSHIP!

COME FIRST *to* ME

You are disobedient, My child, when you listen first to others and then come to Me for a confirmation. I am your Source, and you ought never to look to others until AFTER you have come to Me.

My will brings peace, because My Spirit in you desires always to please Me. Being rightly related to Me is your safeguard. If in all things your foremost desire is to please Me, I will not let you fail.

The Hour *of* Destiny

O My people, draw near to Me and I will speak to your hearts, and you shall know that it is My voice for I shall confirm My word. He who searches for My truth shall be taught of the Lord, and he shall know that the vessel used is chosen and prepared by Me and does not speak of himself, but every word that I shall give him, THAT shall He speak.

I call you again this day, My people, to come to the well and DRINK, and come to My Word and partake. Let the hunger of your soul be nourished by the one source of life which alone can satisfy. No human voice can answer the cry of the soul. My Spirit alone can heal the broken heart and revive the languishing. In mercy I minister. In compassion I deal with your sins. *"Return unto the Lord,"* it is written, *"and He shall have mercy and abundantly pardon."*

I shall have a people purged and prepared for these latter days. My purposes SHALL be fulfilled. MY Church *shall* stand, and truly, the gates of hell shall NOT prevail against its witness in the world. I shall preserve the faithful remnant, and they shall walk with Me in white.

You shall lay aside your own petty personal plans and selfish desires as you grasp the magnitude of the challenge of THIS HOUR. Many are still sleeping who should be AWAKE. Many still toy with trivialities. I plead with you, My people, to seek Me with intensity and with a broken, teachable spirit. I am not asking for your *help* but for your consecration. I need trumpets through which to *sound,* vessels through which to *flow,* hearts through which to *love,* and lips to honor My Name.

Rise up, quit you like men; be strong. Lo, the battle is in array. The enemy takes no rest. Wherever he perceives a point of weakness, your hope of victory is small. I am your strength and your only sure defense. See that you walk in the Spirit. Only then is victory ensured.

Compare not your walk with others. You judge falsely and unwisely. Falsely, because you see not the whole situation, and unwisely because I judge each man individually. Judge your own heart and examine your own way. Condemn not another for his imperfection, but cry unto Me that I may forgive your own iniquity and take away your sin. Make straight paths, and let Me prepare through the desert a highway of holiness and a path of peace.

Lo, the world is both at once on the precipice of destruction and on the brink of revival. It is on the verge of being both consumed by the fires of purification and restored to Edenic perfection. Know the day in which you live, O My people. Listen intently to My voice, for how shall you obey except you know My will and how shall you run except you be sent?

Lay aside the levity that robs the soul of its vitality. Put away the clamour of self-seeking that closes your ear to My voice. Let the zeal of the Lord consume self-pity and the fires of My holiness consume your sins.

Lo, you have not many days to ready your soul. THIS is the hour of your own spiritual destiny, and every present action is laying up in store for you either eternal reward or eternal poverty. He who has been faithful in little shall be entrusted with much, and he who rules well over his own city shall be given authority over ten. I shall not create in that day leaders in the kingdom. I am *preparing* them even now from those few who choose to lay aside the weights of carnal pursuits and cast themselves headlong into full dedication to My will.

THE ABIDING PRESENCE

"No good thing will he withhold from them who walk uprightly" (Psalm 84:11). My presence within you is your richest treasure. It is one that moth and rust cannot destroy, nor thieves break through and steal. It will become dearer to you as you relinquish outer joys. Your inner joy is as a plant that unnurtured fades. Your inner joy is nurtured by your awareness of and gratitude for My abiding presence. Be not allured by the fascinations of the world. They are but to perish. They are transitory. Even those which are not evil are still of no benefit to your spirit.

It is the Word of God and the Spirit of God that feed the soul of a man. It is his inner worship and outer witness that strengthen him in faith. To fail to worship is to become a perpetual disappointment to the heart of Christ. It is to ignore the sacrifice of Calvary. It is to live and die ungrateful for His mercy and love. Worship is the only appropriate gift sinful man can give to a holy God. It is the only fitting expression of the ransomed soul. Nothing can bring greater satisfaction to the heart of God except to teach another soul to do likewise.

ENDURANCE *and* LOVE

Endurance is native to those who love, for to truly love is to continue to love under all circumstances. Man's natural love is often an exchange, a mutual giving and receiving; but God's true holy love will give when there is no exchange, because it does not require reward and is not motivated by gifts.

Love gives because it is its nature to give and so is not a respecter of persons nor conditions. *"A friend loveth at all times,"* and because he does, he endures. He endures hardship, pain, privation, poverty, weariness, misunderstanding, and sacrifice of personal wishes and needs. He endures. He continues to give and continues to love giving, and in so doing he is preserved in the day of adversity.

He is preserved from doubts, fears, and questionings. He is protected against discouragement. He is strengthened in weakness and sustained in trouble. He is invincible. And love is his sustaining force. He endures, for he sees Him who is invisible. . .Him who is the epitome of love, and so he is at one with the Creator and receives a continuing creative power which is the secret of his endurance. To be one with the source is to have an unfailing supply.

So bear cheerfully each day's burden, for it is given to purify the soul. In every trial there burns the Refiner's fire.

The Heavenly Quest

Many heartaches come to those who follow Me. Some are common to all men; others are the direct result of simply being a disciple of one who Himself was called *"a man of sorrows, and acquainted with grief"* (Isaiah 53:3). He who is obedient to Me will experience a similar kind of suffering. It is the suffering of spiritual sacrifice. It is not self-sacrifice, for it is not a giving of self, per se. It is a new and more stringent kind of dedication—it is the heavenly quest for total abandonment to the will of God.

POINT *of* REFERENCE

Understanding is the flowering of love, for love opens the eyes of the soul to the realities of the universe. Greatness is hidden from the miserly, and his horizons are shrunken by his selfishness. To love is to learn to be generous, and generosity opens the windows of heaven, not only allowing God to pour out His blessing, but also granting the giver the privilege of looking beyond his human littleness and glimpsing a bit of eternal glory in the light of which all the treasures of earth are as a grain of sand.

Revelation of truth generates from love, because it is love that prompts generosity. He who saves his life shall lose it, and he who gives his life in dedication to Christ discovers that he has preserved that which otherwise he would have selfishly destroyed.

It is not in man's power to protect himself from destruction, for his very desire to do so is an expression of self-love. It is the hand of God Himself that guards the soul of him who pours out his life in full commitment to the claims of Christ. Was it not Christ Himself who poured out His own life in total sacrifice? And was it not love that brought Him to Calvary?

And so it is the secret of the universe. . .to love and to

give. To empty the heart of greed is to disengage the life forces from the destructive bondage of selfishness and free the soul into the liberty of the Spirit. For the Spirit of God is never entangled in human selfishness, and the child of God finds turmoil or peace to the degree that he has loosed himself from the tyranny of his carnal desires. Heaven is open to the worshiper, and in true worship the heart of man is transformed by the love of God. God becomes his point of reference, and the demands of self are silenced.

PATIENCE WAITS

Patience is like the petals of a rose unfolding. It is silent. It does not complain about its own slowness nor chide another for his. It is able to wait, for it knows that time is as important as speed. It knows that there is often much speed in the Spirit while there is slowness in the flesh. It knows there is a divine clock that has wings where man's clock has hands. It is aware of God's perfect timing even though it cannot tell the hour. It penetrates the wall of silence and has faith that God is indeed working even though it does not hear the chiming of the passing hours. Yes, Patience is another child of love; for it is Love that waits, knowing all is well and all WILL be well, because God loves and cares.

Patience can wait because Patience knows that God is Love, and love is timeless, and love is loving while patience is waiting.

Nothing Shall Separate Me

O God; Thy love is as a fire burning in my soul. When I think of Thee in the night seasons, Thou art as a refreshing shower. When I awaken in the morning, my first awareness is of Thy presence. My soul delights in Thy company, and Thy words are unto me as sustaining food.

Never have I been comfortless since Thou hast come to me in the person of Thy Holy Spirit. Never have I thirsted since Thou gavest me this Living Water. Thy countenance has been my sunshine. Thy love has kept my heart tender. I am not left to grope in the dark, but Thou guidest me with Thine eye, and with Thine hand upon my shoulder Thou restrainest me.

The sky shall be rolled up as a curtain. The stars shall be cast down as falling snow. The elements shall melt with fervent heat. Kingdoms shall be destroyed; but Thou, O My God, remainest forever, and I am held in Thy hand. Nothing shall separate me from the love of God!

THE KINGDOM *of* LIGHT

My righteousness, saith the Lord, endures forever. My truth is unchangeable. All generations have looked to Me; they have looked to Me and found strength. My counsels are just; My judgements are holy. Where can man look for a standard of holiness? It is I, the Lord, who set up the standard. My judgements are in equity. Why do you grope in darkness, seeking the light? I am the light; yea, I am the light that lights every man that comes into the world. I am the Lord, your God, who changes not; neither hold I My anger when wickedness rises to destroy the godly. I am a shield to those who put their trust in Me, and the faith of the righteous shall be rewarded.

Do not fear darkness: Fear God, and He shall be to you a light. The world is enshrouded in darkness, but they who walk in My truth walk in light. From every place where the Word is spoken, LIGHT goes forth into the hearts of men. My Spirit will give you discernment to see either the light or the darkness hidden in other hearts, that you may witness in wisdom. For the light of the Spirit is seen in the Spirit, and My people shall thus recognize one another. Some there are who profess to be Mine and are not. He who sees in the Spirit will not be deceived. My

Spirit will teach you, and you must learn rapidly, for the days are short. Deception is everywhere. Blindness and destruction walk together. My kingdom is a kingdom of light, and clear, purified vessels are the transmitters of My glory in the darkened world. SHINE, My children, and darkness shall be scattered as you walk!

THE GOLDEN BRIDGE

Lose all else, if need be, but do not lose My nearness. In conscious union with Me there is rest and quietness of soul. There is a golden bridge formed between us by our love for each other. It is stronger than steel.

Make *a* New Commitment

My Spirit will not always strive. If by rebellion you resist My overtures, I will release you to your own way and you may walk alone if that is your choice. I have made free will a gift, and I will not violate your right to follow your own desires. Better not to start to follow Me than to be a deserter. Nothing can compensate for the loss of My favor. The beggar at the rich man's gate fared better in afterlife than the master of the house, for he was escorted by angels to the comfort of Paradise.

Life is fleeting, and the rewards are sure, whether good or bad. The end is in My hands; the preparation in yours. Do not compromise your victory by moments of denial. These may not be recognized as such except under the light of the Spirit's discerning. You can fail Me a thousand times and be unaware unless you are sensitive and open to the convicting work of My Holy Spirit. Belshazzar was pleased with himself until he heard the words of the handwriting on the wall. Uzzah thought to do good when he steadied the ark and forfeited his life by his act of disobedience.

Only My Word and My Spirit can hold your soul in purity, and so you must continually expose your own spirit to their influence. To abide in Christ is to abide in holiness, and there is no other way. To abide in good works is not enough. To abide in good intentions is to fail. To rely on your own intellect is certain disaster. To trust Me as a little child trusts his father is the only safe way. Have I asked so hard a thing? To pride, it is hard. To love, it is easy. Let Me melt your heart anew, and let Me restore your spiritual vitality.

I have waited for you with patience, but I beg you to turn to Me speedily, for truly the hour is late and much remains unfinished. Make a new commitment, and I will bestow a fresh anointing and we shall rejoice together beyond anything in the past.

Rise Up! For the labourers are few.

MERCY *and* GRACE

Mercy is the grace of the forgiven. It is possible to give only that which has been received. The man who has not accepted his own forgiveness cannot extend forgiveness to his brother.

It is the nature of mercy to be gracious. Grace forgives and in so doing unlocks the self-condemned from his prison of guilt. This law operates between God and man and between man and his brother. What you loose on earth, said Jesus, shall be loosed in heaven; and likewise, what you bind on earth shall be bound in heaven.

Any resentment harbored toward a brother is a binding force upon his soul. He may take authority over it and free himself, or he may fail to recognize the source of his bondage and continue in torment. Evil thoughts toward others would be dealt with swiftly if the extent of their damaging influence were even dimly understood. Furthermore, the harmful impact is equally destructive to both the sender and the receiver—the offending and the offended. For the force of evil, as the force of good, oper-ates in a spiritually tangible way as powerfully as if it were translated into words or deeds. This is why Jesus said in effect, "The law says, do not kill, but I say, do not hate." A man cannot be prosecuted by civil law for wrong thoughts; but in the courts of heaven, his guilt is sealed while his sin is yet only a mental crime. Many a would-be saint has lost communion with his heavenly Father and forfeited inner peace because of hate, resentment, and unforgiveness, even when these thoughts have been concealed in the innermost recesses of his heart.

It is the work of the Holy Spirit, the purger of souls, to ferret out these enemies of the love of Christ, to bring insight and conviction and guide the offender to repentance and forgiveness. At this point, the love of Christ takes over and begins to teach him how to redirect his thoughts into channels of love, forgiveness, and grace. He will learn how to free and not to bind; how to send a blessing rather than a curse; how to pray constructively rather than to condemn an erring brother.

So shall God's people be healed and His Church prosper because Grace shall flow from member to member, binding breaches and pouring oil upon troubled waters; opening the door for the return of the prodigal and encouraging the fainthearted.

THE SEARCHER *and the* FINDER

Freedom in the Spirit is a gift to those who renounce all else but God. God is not religion, and God is not self-realization. God is not personal happiness, and God is not the end of searching.

The Searcher may die still a searcher. It is hopeless to look for God and expect to find Him, or to seek peace and joy, for all this is a *gift*. Gifts are not found or attained. Gifts are received. Some have been so busy seeking that they have disdained the quietness and unpretentiousness of a Finder.

No one can tell the Seeker how to cease to be a Seeker and become a Finder because the Seeker is deaf to all but the sound of his own voice. It is as though he believed his shouting would inevitably be heard. The only reward of protest is increasing resentment in the protesting, for it is a denial of My Spirit, and by such action guilt is intensified and true peace is postponed.

MOVE *in* FAITH

I said that all things are possible to him who believes. Can you accept this? Can you move in faith, anticipating that the mountain truly shall be removed?

Do we not labor together, and if I am with you, how can you fail? To doubt is to ignore My presence and in failing to reckon on My power you are thrown upon your own resources, and when you are thrown upon your own resources, you are immediately conscious of limitations, and as soon as you feel your own limitations you fear failure, and when you fear failure you create an atmosphere that precludes the operation of omnipotence. You are wholly cast upon the arm of flesh and thus doomed to fail.

Turn unto Me. Fasten your confidence in Me. Give Me time and liberty to work—you will never be disappointed, for he who trusts in Me shall be comforted. He shall be blessed above his fellows and rewarded beyond his expectation, for I look for faith and rejoice when I find it.

HOLY LOVE

When you listen to My voice, My child, you are loving Me. Love in its highest form is communication of lofty thoughts. Holy love does not demand personal attention. When two human hearts mingle in worship to Me, their ardor rises as the fragrance of incense, bringing joy to My heart. This is the sublimest expression of human love. It takes nothing and gives all and receives from My own hand the reward. For there is a reward for worship; indeed, there are many rewards, and they are of the wealth of heaven and are untarnishable and can never be lost.

The first is peace of soul; for holy love silences the demands of the flesh man. When holy love rises to My throne, it releases a golden river of grace which floods the hearts of those who thus love Me and overflows to others for whom they pray.

Rest of soul is joy in its purest form. Absence of inner peace causes common moments of joy to be fleeting. Lasting joy evades the selfish, and peace eludes the unyielded, because the motivations are contrary to My purposes, and the goals sought do not glorify Me.

Obedience, *the* Fabric *of* Happiness

"The Lord is my light and my salvation. The Lord is the strength of my life" (from Psalm 27:1).

Failure to respond to My love causes depression of spirit. No soul is strong enough to survive the struggles of life triumphantly without divine aid. It is My strength imparted to the weak which causes him to rise up and walk in strength. It is My joy filling the broken heart that gives a song to displace mourning.

Look to Me, My child, and all your needs will be met by My abundant provision. I will not suffer the enemy to overthrow him who puts his confidence in Me. I am faithful to My Word, and I have promised never to fail nor to forsake.

Doubt is of the devil: give it no place. Fear is paralyzing: Refuse to entertain it.

Obedience is the fabric of happiness. To rebel is to seek sorrow. Only a yielded heart can find rest in Me; and to know contentment there must be resignation of personal rights in favor of My will.

RELATE *to* ME

There is a quiet place of communion in the center of My will. It is not given you to see all the actions that bear upon your life. Many influences affect your every thought. You need the quiet time with Me to lift you above the swirling winds of the voices of other people and give you the true direction of My Spirit. Man has not the wisdom to direct his own way, nor one man to lead another. My Spirit shall direct you, My hand shall guide you and I will bring peace.

Turmoil comes from reacting to people. Peace is born of response to My Spirit. There is harmony of soul for those who are in tune with Me. Listening to the false sounds of man will put you in tune with man. He who would be in tune with heaven must hear the tone of My voice. Man clamours for your attention: I wait until your own desire draws you aside. Man demands recognition: I wait for your love. Loving Me will release you from the demands of your own and other men's egos. Loving Me will give you direction when those around you are losing their way. Relate to Me. As you relate first to Me, I will help you to rightly relate to others.

Darkness is related to light. God made the evening

and the morning and He called it a day. Your experience is a daily combination of evening and morning—darkness and light. Man brings you darkness; I bring you light. Man brings distraction; I bring unity. Man separates; I gather. Man destroys; I give life. I created the darkness as well as the light. You will learn in both. *"The day and the night are both alike to Me"* (Psalm 139:12). This is because My light penetrates the darkness. This will become true in your own walk of faith as My understanding enlightens your own heart and ignorance gives way to the illumination of My Spirit.

LIFE *of* DISCOVERY

Virtue will flow, My child, from the hem of *your* garment as it flowed from Mine, as you allow My life within you to have dominance. My Spirit indwells you, not for your own edification alone, but for the blessing of others, as well. Do not hinder the flow.

It is your love for Me that increases your capacity to receive freely My virtue. My "virtue" is the full orb of My total personality. It is only the beginning of your life in the Spirit when you receive forgiveness and salvation. That is your *entrance* into life eternal. There is more. . .and more. . . and more. You have by grace and faith been birthed into an ever unfolding, ever expanding life of discovery; for you have been destined by My will to enter into My glory.

It is not that you were saved only to enter some day into heaven. No, you have been redeemed at great price that you should enter NOW in your daily life into the position of sonship: the responsibilities and the privileges of the identification of your own new inner man with the Spirit of Christ.

Prepare!

My child, think of the future as being yours *now*, for in Me all time is Present. Procrastination, fear of the unknown, preoccupation with the present and many other hindrances to progress will cease to exist for you when you embrace the future *in Me*.

Your own future is shaped by today's decisions, therefore the future should not be ignored as though irrelevant to today. Jesus did not teach man to *ignore the future*, but to *prepare* for it. His warning was against *anxiety* concerning tomorrow, not against *preparation*.

It was I who taught Noah to prepare for the flood (Genesis 6:13–22). I gave Joseph wisdom as to how to prepare for the seven-year famine (Genesis 41). I showed Gideon how to prepare his army in advance of the battle (Judges 7). The message of John the Baptist was a message of preparation: *"Prepare ye the way of the LORD"* (Isaiah 40:3). I have taught you to be prepared for the second coming (Matthew 24:44).

Yes, the riches of the future are for those who make preparation today. Draw on My wisdom, for to Me all things are plain now.

RESURRECTION LIFE

My peace is yours, surrounding and supporting you. You may think My *strength* supports you, but it is actually My *peace* that makes you strong, because only the heart at rest can receive My life-flow. Many suffer bodily ills because their tension makes it impossible for them to receive life from Me.

I am constantly pouring out My life upon My children as the sun pours its rays upon the flowers, but the secret of receiving lies in the exposure. The flower concealed from the sun receives no light. It is the same with the soul. Tension becomes like a covering which shuts out My peace from the total person—body, soul, and spirit, and produces illness in all these areas.

Wait upon Me in love and worship. Open your soul. My Spirit restores and revives. Resurrection life is your portion, and it becomes yours as you expose your soul to My love and light.

A Rain *of* Fire

O My children, it is a rain of fire that is falling. It is a rain of judgement upon My house; for the Scripture says, if judgement must begin at the house of God, what shall be the end of the ungodly and the sinner? (1 Peter 4:17). It is My people whom I am purifying now, and I must purge out the dross. . .the chaff of indifference, the impurities of self-seeking, and the rottenness of rebellion.

My house must again become a house of prayer and a place of worship. My temple must be a place where My children seek My face and give Me their devotion. My altars must be a place for the confession of sin, and your tears must be tears of repentance.

Too long have you curried favor of one another. Too long have you condemned the faults in your brother and ignored your own. Too long have you sought to cover your sins. But I say unto you: The Fire shall search them out. Yes, it shall search out and burn the chaff, and it shall burn the wood. It shall devour the endeavors of the flesh that have passed as devotion. It shall consume every word that is not true, and it shall reveal that which is genuine. For when all that is valueless is removed, then shall the jewels of reality shine forth in their beauty and splendor.

For I have wrought in your lives by My Spirit, says the Lord, and that which I have done is perfect. It shall not be concealed in the day of purification. It shall be unveiled and revealed by the fire—for the fire shall test all things, whether or not they are true work of God.

You cannot do this work yourself. It is My work. I shall send the fire as you wait upon Me. It shall bring you refreshing as a rain. It shall be death to the old carnal nature, but it shall be life to the inner man—the new nature that is yours in Christ.

Never be afraid of My judgements. I do not send them in wrath upon My Church, but in love and compassion. I have bound Myself by My Word to meet all your needs, and you have need of cleansing and purification. Can I abandon you to your sin? Knowing the beauty that lies buried within you, as the pearl was hid in the field, can I be true to My love for you and remain indifferent to your imperfection?

No, for My wisdom and My love and My holiness are all working together with My saving power to bring you to perfection. My Church is dear to My heart: or have you forgotten that you are Mine? Have you lost sight of the fact that you were *created* by My Spirit? Shall I not *PERFECT* all that which I begin?

I shall gather to Myself a people who have been tried in the fire—yes, a furnace heated seven times. They shall be Mine in that day when I shall come to snatch away My jewels. Is this not what a thief seeks in the night? He does not look for that which is valueless. This is why the Scripture says I come as a thief in the night. I am coming to snatch My precious gems. For the day was when you were the possession of the enemy of your souls, even Satan himself. You were "sold under sin." But he shall not detain you when I come for you. For the strong man may guard the house, but when a stronger man than he shall come, He shall overcome him (Mark 3:27).

To Feel Need Is *to* Receive Grace

My mercy flows in the stream of all your woes, My child. No obstacle within yourself can restrict My grace. I love you when you cannot love yourself. I forgive you while you are still repenting. I am blessing you while you are still pleading for mercy. I am not thwarted by your unperfected expression. I use many vessels while they are struggling with their failures; for in their conscious sense of need, they are more yielded to Me than they who think themselves to be without flaw. In truth, nothing restricts the Spirit's work more than the smug satisfaction of the spiritually proud who sense no lack and who neither are repenting nor calling for aid.

To feel need is to receive grace. *"Call unto me, and I will answer thee, and show thee great and mighty things, which thou knowest not"* (Jeremiah 33:3). Yes, the mighty things which you do not comprehend are the miraculous things which I do for you and through you in your *acknowledged times of need,* and they are beyond your understanding and greater than your ability; for I act in and through you according to My grace and My own ability.

I WILL SHARE *with* YOU MY SECRETS

I will share with you My secrets
And reveal the hidden thing.
I will lift you out of darkness—
Understanding will I bring.
If you seek Me in My fulness
And desire to know My heart,
I will open heaven's riches
And My wisdom I'll impart.
I have not ordained My children
To be blind, uncomprehending:
I will be the light eternal,
Revelation to you sending.
For 'twas sin that brought the darkness,
And 'tis sin that blinds the soul,
But the blood of the atonement
Opens eyes and makes men whole.

DANIEL 2:22

F J R

LIGHT *of* LIFE

Alleluia, Christ is risen,
He is risen from the tomb.
He has baffled powers of evil,
Conquered darkness, sin and gloom.

He is ris'n, o'er death victorious,
Ris'n triumphant o'er the grave;
All the powers of hell are shaken,
The Redeemer lives to save.

See Him in ascended glory.
What a wond'rous, radiant sight!
Prophecy has found fulfillment,
Christ is LIFE, and He is LIGHT.

Light that conquers all earth's darkness,
Light that bids all fear depart,
Light revealing God's great mercy,
LIGHT of LIFE within my heart!

F J R

CALLED *to* PRAISE

Have I not promised to care for you, yes, indeed have I not done so and faithfully, lo, these many years? Are you fearful now when distress is all about? Rest your heart in Me and draw courage from My Word. *"It is vain for you to rise up early and sit up late and eat the bread of sorrow,"* wrote the poet of old (Psalm 127:2).

I have not called you to lamentation but to PRAISE. This should be your foremost occupation at all times. This should be your greatest joy, as it is your chief duty. You will find in praise the fountainhead of spiritual understanding and strength, for My Spirit saturates the soul that learns to pour itself out in worship, and that one becomes the object of My love and My instruction. YOU may be that one, My child!

The Glory *of* Identification

I have freed you from sin, My child, by the power of My shed blood, for I hung upon the cross as the substitutional sacrifice in your place. For it is written, *"the soul that sinneth, it shall die"* (Ezekiel 18:4), so the sentence of death was passed upon every mortal soul, for all have sinned and come short of the glory of God. Yes, only to have lost the glory light in which the first Adam was created when he came pure from My hand is to fall short of the glory of God, and as Adam sinned and lost that glory, he led the entire human race into the experience of spiritual darkness. For in his fall from the state of innocence, he lost the glory of his initial communion or identification with Me, his creator. In the breaking of My word to him, he lost his glory walk with Me.

I say unto you, if you would enter into the glory of identification with Me, you must once again come into a place of trust and obedience, and submission to My sovereign authority. And it is through the shed blood that this restoration is possible. It is not by any good works of your own, for a multitude of good deeds cannot wash away the stain of sin nor restore broken fellowship.

Forgiveness is in the atonement, and the atonement is by

the sacrifice of the holy, spotless Lamb of God. Apart from this, there is no salvation, no redemption, no cleansing, no forgiveness. Never forget the price that was paid for your eternal life. Apart from the shed blood, there is only death, judgement, and hell for every soul. I am the Lord, your God, and beside Me there is no other. He who believes in Me shall never die, and he who comes to Me for life shall never perish.

PENITENCE RESTORES

You are the child of My love, and it is My desire to bless. Come not unto Me in timidity. To doubt is to fear, and he who fears cannot receive My help. My grace is not limited by human flaws. It is need, not worthiness, that draws My response.

I am as eager to sustain as you are desirous of strength. If your weakness brings you to the mercy seat, it is an instrument of good. You are better able to worship Me when you have conscious need. Self-righteousness destroys the heart as a moth eats a garment. Penitence restores, and peace rules where self-abandonment provides a place.

Ignorance is folly, and wisdom without tolerance is cruel. Seek wisdom; but in searching, lose not simplicity, for wisdom without simplicity is a snare. A little wisdom puffs up; let him who considers himself wise know that a pure heart and reverence for God are the beginning of understanding. The heart of a child is an open vessel for mercy because he has not erected artifices to protect his self-esteem. The prayer of the child is answered because of its unvarnished simplicity.

Procrastination precludes deliverance, because it seeks My blessings today while refusing to accept them until tomorrow. No hindrance warrants discouragement; for I will comfort the mourner, cause the lame to walk, and I will heal the breach.

THE SINGLE EYE

To turn from sin, My child, is an easy thing to do if your eye is single and your heart is fixed on Me. The enticement of sin will easily lure the simple; but the wise know that it is the way of death.

To walk in darkness is folly, but the pure of heart will seek the paths of righteousness.

DELIVER US *from* EVIL

You will never be strong, My child, as long as you lean upon your own arm of flesh, for within you lie areas of weakness. You will become strong only as you depend on Me to be your fortitude and your protection. Fortitude will give you inner peace, and My protection shields you from the attacks of others that rise to attempt to destroy.

You will move without fear into the position of resisting the oppression of the unjust man when you see Me as the victor. It is not so important that YOU be stronger than the opposition. *The victory lies in knowing that I am stronger.* Knowing this will give you strength when you have no strength and will rout fear from your heart. Keeping your thoughts on ME will divert your attention from the difficulty and cause courage to rise in your heart in the face of danger.

I was never in fear; therefore I was able to answer wisely when My enemies set about to destroy Me. You can do the same when you draw on My Spirit for your defense and your deliverance from evil.

Kingdom Preparation

My people, hear My word: This hour is exceedingly strategic. *Every move* you make needs to be directed by My Holy Spirit. Every action performed can tell for eternity if you are doing those things that I put on your heart to do. And that which is OMITTED of the things I ask you to do and say grieves Me, because only I know how much more would have been accomplished for My kingdom if you had been faithful and obedient.

GO when I send you and SPEAK the words I give you to speak. *I* shall bring the increase. Do not any longer thwart My purposes by lack of courage and thoughts of personal limitations. It is MY WORKS and MY WORDS that are powerful and effective, and you have only to get self out of the way and all concern about your own weak vessel, and let Me move *through* you to accomplish My purposes.

You know these things already. I am pleading with you to *let it happen,* not particularly for the sake of what you personally can experience, but because of the desperate need of this hour for My will to be brought to pass in hearts and lives to which you have access, and thus to whom YOU have a responsibility.

I need you! If you could begin to grasp this fact, you

would overcome your hesitancy and forever be freed from all the fears about your personal inadequacies that have plagued you for so long. It is not a lack of love for Me that holds you back. It is specifically the fact that you do not yet fully realize that any deed I direct you to do and any word I give you to speak has power beyond your comprehension. I Myself vitalize and "dynamize" all My own action. All My own actions and words are Almighty, and they are so as they move through you. Sometimes I have kept this reality veiled from My servants because I know the weakness of mortal flesh and the temptation in man to take unto himself the glory, and I know the danger both to man himself and to My cause if he does not truly know that ALL the power in this action is GOD, rather than himself. But I am pleading with you because of the need of the hour to let this power flow through you as you have never done before, for MY work right now is like the critical moments at the crisis hour of a great battle.

This is a crucial hour in spiritual conflict for the forces of evil and of righteousness in the world. If all this were visible to you as it is to Me, you would NEVER get in My way because of personal thoughts, for the very excitement of your true comprehension would save you from all self-consciousness and self-preservation.

PRAY until you begin to receive some of this spiritual enlightenment and can feel with Me the urgency and the danger and the deadly seriousness of this hour. From that point on, you will flow with Me, move with Me, and work with Me. Many victories can still be won and much force can be exerted to thwart the enemy and hasten the coming of My kingdom.

Man shall never achieve the kingdom alone; but lo, I say unto you, neither can I except as I am able to move through My people. There is no other way. This is the only hope. The present generation has a fearful responsibility to the human race, for to this generation has been committed the momentous task of Kingdom Preparation. Hear Me, My chosen ones, and pray for further enlightenment.

HERITAGE *of the* GODLY

O My child, when you listen to Me in any circumstance, I will bring light and understanding. I will bring peace; for it is by My Spirit that all things are accomplished. It is by your faith and prayer that you become receptive to the moving of My Spirit. I do not enter the scene to cause disturbance but to bring into focus the truth that will set you free.

You have no reason to be anxious nor to strive. You have nothing to lose and everything to gain; for he who follows Me can never be desolate.

Be careful that you are following Me, and I will care for all else. *"The servant of God must not strive"* (2 Timothy 2:24). Striving is for those who have not yet learned to trust Me. Anxiety is the affliction of the self-possessed. The godly know their heritage and revel in the protection of their Redeemer. For it is in the blood of Jesus that refuge is found for every onslaught of the enemy.

The Labor That Wearies

There is a labor that is weariness to the spirit. You are in danger of this kind of action whenever you move under the impulse of outside forces. Response to My Spirit within will result in outer peace. You are in harmony with the outer when you are in tune within. To respond to the demands of outside forces injects hostile influences into the soul.

To be at peace with Me in your own heart, you must close the door firmly to the entrance of every alien intruder. If you carelessly allow entrance, you invite chaos, and it is you who will pay the penalty.

To guard your own peace is easier than to try to regain it after it has been lost. It is the work of regaining it that I have called "the labor that wearies the Spirit." It is not only tiring, but time-consuming. You cannot afford the luxury of wasted time. The King's business is too important to wait while you make reparation for your mistakes which could have been avoided.

Determine not to repeat your folly.

The Spirit's Shield

Only in the release of the seen do you lay hold on the unseen, My little one. Heaven waits for those who are no longer bound to earth. The degree to which bondages are exchanged for liberties while still in the flesh is in proportion to the extent to which eternal values are held in higher esteem than worldly success and possessions. If a man loves Me, he will hold his soul more precious than his body and will pursue holiness at the expense of wealth; for to follow after that which perishes is to forfeit the prize of the high calling in Christ.

There is no place in the kingdom of heaven for a divided heart. It is in the division that love is lost; and to lose My love, My child, is to lose what cannot be regained. For a loving heart is a vessel of light and mercy. It is a receptacle into which I pour My grace. It is untarnished by avarice and indifferent to the call of worldly ambition.

To be united with Me in total dedication to My highest will protects the soul from forces of destruction. There is no safety in external circumstances. The only shield for the spirit of a man is My presence. It is written,

"The angel of the LORD encampeth round about them that fear him, and delivereth them" (Psalm 34:7). This is your safe-keeping, My child, and My love is your reward.

CHRIST REQUIRES OBEDIENCE

When Christ was here, He was looking for disciples. . . He still is looking for them today. Man searches for leaders; Jesus seeks followers. Man elevates the educated; Christ blesses the teachable. Man struggles for power; Christ teaches submission. Man strives for prestige; the Holy Spirit produces humility. Man labors for achievement; Christ requires only obedience.

FINDING *the* CONSTANT

You are ever in My care, My child. As the entire universe is kept in motion by My sovereign power, so I guide the destinies of your life, and it is by My hand that the course of nature is controlled. I do not overrule your free will, but as you yield your will to Me, I guard you from actions that would work contrary to My purposes. You can walk confidently into each day with assurance of My protection and provision. Your heart can be at peace in the wildest storm. For he whose treasure lies in heaven fears no loss. Remember where your treasure is and earthly things will lose their power to touch your peace. I am your peace. I am your security. I am your support.

Fears rise out of selfish desires. He who desires only to please Me frees his soul from worldly cares. He is content to receive whatever good may come, and he can release whatever he possesses and feel no loss. In every experience, either receiving or giving, he feels neither richer nor poorer. He has found a CONSTANT. Christ is his all in all. All else comes and goes as clouds moving across the sky. He sees the change but is not disturbed by the action. So is every man who counts not his life dear unto himself. Such is he who has made heaven his home and the eternal God his refuge; for he abides in the secret place of the Most High, and his life is hid with Christ in God.

The Ultimate Cure

My presence is experienced not by how you *feel,* but how you *believe.* It is your *trust* that brings you near to Me. I am always with you, as I promised I would be. Your *awareness* of My presence is in proportion to your confidence in Me.

If you find it difficult to trust, then LOVE Me. Love bridges every gap and leaps over every mountain. It is the ultimate cure for every ill.

Journey *in the* Spirit

Your first thoughts in the morning should be of Me, your heavenly Father. It is I who have kept you through the night and am giving you this fresh new day. I have surprises awaiting you which you need My guidance not to miss.

It will become a joyful experience to walk with Me through every day as you make it a habit to join your heart to Mine before you set out on the day's journeys. The day's journey may take you no further than your doorstep, yes, for some who are confined by illness, their journeys will be only in the Spirit, but all may be beautiful, for the spirits that are identified with Me and expressing My life-thoughts travel with Me though they go nowhere. He who travels much without Me is truly the one who goes nowhere, for all his activity is of no eternal consequence.

The earthly life is like a bank into which deposits may be made for future fulfillment. All the rewards of earth are transitory. This is why Jesus said, "They have their reward," speaking of the men who sought and received the passing praises of men. Those who do not seek the praise of men but who seek only to please Me lay up eternal reward for the life beyond, which reward is of far greater value.

Indeed, he who has little faith in the next world will scarcely be interested in deferring his blessings for that future time. He will be a "bird-in-hand" follower. More correctly, he is a bird-in-hand deserter; for the very state of mind which causes a man to prefer earthly joys before heavenly joys marks him as a child of time and place and disqualifies him for true spiritual expression.

REFLECT MY LOVE

This is My day, says the Lord. There are no shadows in My light. There are no storms in My heart. There is only peace, rest, and holy love for you, My child, if you will walk in My Spirit and reflect My love. I do not ask a difficult thing. I offer you the treasures of My heart to adorn your countenance as one would wear a jewel to adorn the body. As Scriptures say, a woman is not adorned by pearls, but by a meek and quiet spirit.

Let this be your secret weapon against any enemy that may beset you today. Be concerned that I may glorify Myself and take no thought of your own personal gain or loss or welfare. Accept what comes as a gift from My hand and know that I make all things work together for good. My good is your best. Receive it with joy. I am able to take a crumb and fill the world with bread. I have given you what you possess, and I am able to multiply it as the needs arise and at the most advantageous times.

Trust Me and all shall be well.

CULTIVATE LOVE

Your attention, My child, is important to Me. If you do not give Me a listening ear, I cannot speak to you. If I cannot communicate with you, we lose our rapport. It is on the basis of fellowship that love is nurtured, and to neglect to cultivate love is to ultimately destroy it, for it is not self-sustaining. It is like the dawning of the morning and he who sleeps has missed it forever. There is no other avenue through which the spirit may be sustained in grace. Time spent in worship is imperative. The results are not to be gained in any other form of expression. He who spends much time in worship is ministered to in the Spirit in ways that are inscrutable.

THE ROBE *of* HUMILITY

I come to you, My child, in many different ways, some of which are apparent to you and others of which you are unaware. It is in discovering these that you will be enriched with a deeper sense of My love for you and My nearness to you.

I am involved in every action that touches your life and every action in which your life touches another life. I do not demand from you perfect performance; but I desire that you have a right response to the need of others, and that your own outreach toward Me shall be a faith action.

To pray and not believe is a mockery. To respond negatively to your brother's need is a repudiation of My love.

Some souls are enhanced by suffering. Others are embittered by grief. One can lift a song in the night. Others cannot breathe a prayer at midday. To reprove, but not condemn, to lift a fallen brother without exhibiting disapproval. . .this rejoices My heart. For I came not to condemn, but to save; not to resent man's inherent weakness, but to reinstate him in My grace and forgiveness.

You cannot effectively minister until you lay aside the cloak of spiritual superiority and walk in the robe of true humility. Everywhere, and in all things, as I have freely given to you, so must you also freely give to others—not for reward nor for approval. If in secret you bless another, your soul will be enriched; for it is in so doing that in truth you give to *Me,* and it shall be from *ME* that you will receive the reward.

QUIETNESS *of* SOUL

Your heart is Mine for I have made it My dwelling place. Your peace is in knowing at all times that I abide within the secret places of your soul. When you are plunged "beyond your depth," know that whatever you are experiencing, My love is as a deep pool in your heart. See your pain and your fear as dropping into that pool and being engulfed in My all-sufficient grace. Having learned this secret, nothing can intimidate you from without, and nothing can distress you from within.

I am not concerned with externals, for it is the hidden life in the Spirit of a man that determines his destiny. There are winds that blow upon the face of the earth. They are the capricious winds of fate. They do not blow upon the inner man nor do they disturb his peace. Quietness of soul is vital to spiritual health because unrest muffles the still, small voice of My Spirit.

PATIENCE IS BORN *of* LOVE

Patience is born of love, and he who has learned to love shall have no need to pray for patience for he has within himself the root that produces this fruit. Love is the source of many other virtues, for God is love and love is an expression of God, and in Him dwell all the virtues. To lack love and pray for patience is futile, for patience is a fruit borne on the tree of love. *"He that loveth is born of God and he that loveth not knoweth not God, for God is love"* (1 John 4:7–8). Beloved, believe not every spirit, but try the spirits. . . . TEST the spirit of a man. And by what shall he be tested? He shall be tested by love.

He who does not express love exposes the darkness of his soul, though he be clothed with religion. "This man's religion is vain," wrote James, if he does not show concern for the needy and pity for the widow (James 1:26–27) and if he does not express his faith by kindness and good deeds. He needs no man to condemn him; he condemns himself by his failure to show consideration for the feelings of his brother. No amount of pious platitudes can outweigh his guilt. He has appointed himself to a high place and is scarcely fit for the lowest.

"But he that is greatest among you shall be your servant,"

said Jesus (Matthew 23:11).

You seek acceptance, forgetting that Jesus was despised and rejected.

You seek happiness, ignoring the fact that He was a man of sorrows and knew much grief.

You seek security, when the Son of Man had no certain place to lay His head.

You seek fame, whereas He sought obscurity.

You seek honor, when He was spit upon and scourged.

And why do you seek falsely? It is because you have not learned to love. Love changes all the desires. Love knows that doing the Father's will is the only thing of value. Because love does not seek its own, it is not dismayed when circumstances are unfavorable. Love is never haughty nor ill-tempered. Love will tolerate disrespect and not be offended, because it does not demand recognition and approval.

To be fleet of foot and keen of mind will only lead more quickly to disaster if love is lacking. Love is the source of joy, and it is the heart of culture. He who has love will be a gentleman though he be untaught in social graces. He will be a diplomat out of consideration for others and not for personal advantage. He will labor happily though unremunerated and sacrifice personal comfort without protest or complaint. He will measure happiness by his power to give and weakness by his limitation to bring comfort to those in need.

Yes, love is the touchstone of all meaningful human expression.

GUIDANCE

He who desires only to do his own will shall never experience divine guidance. My guidance is given in response to a desire to please Me. He who wishes to please himself will not enquire as to how to please Me.

I REQUIRE FAITHFULNESS

It is faithfulness which I require above all else. When you are faithful in little things, I will increase your responsibilities and with the increase I will enlarge your capacity to understand. You will fail many times, but you will rise again and overcome the next time, because in each experience of failure you are being taught the right way and the wrong way. When you know the right way and choose the right way, then you will be spared disappointments. Disappointments come because of your carelessness and imprudence. It is not something strange that a matter should turn out for ill. It is rather to be expected because of the ways of the world. Do not blame yourself. You had faith, but the faith was misplaced. You lacked experience. This you are getting. It is always expensive!

Wait on Me. I will show you the solution. I will help you in this as I have helped you in other things. Do not fear nor mourn your plight. Trust ME to give you guidance. I see all things and I will right the wrong and show you My way to solve the problem.

Do not fear, I say, for confidence will bring you aid, but fear will lead to confusion. You need always to be strong for the sake of others as well as yourself. Come to Me with ALL your problems. As you look to Me I will help you find the solution. You are disappointed because *people* have failed you and betrayed your confidence. Do not be surprised. My children fail Me over and over—even when they are desiring to do good and please Me. Whenever you depend on people you can expect disappointments. *Your response* is what I am watching. By wrong actions they have failed you, but *by wrong reaction you can fail Me* and that is the worse of the two. You have enough problems already. Care first for your own immediate concerns. Give this to Me.

Let Me have it and do not grieve your soul. Deliberately set your attention on other matters, and while you are trusting Me, I will take care of it in My own way. Believe, trust, wait, and see My hand work.

Preparation *and* Restoration

My glory is hidden from the eye that is filled with the world. For the world is passing away with all its allurement, but the Lord your God hovers over His children to bring forth a people who shall share His glory. He will not be detained by the actions of men. Man exalts himself and creates for himself prominence. It is nothing in My sight, says the Lord. For I raise up, and I put down, and the day approaches when all the kingdoms of the world shall be the kingdom of the Lord, the God of heaven, and He shall reign forever and ever.

What a hope you have, My children! For in that day, you shall reign with Me, if indeed you are willing now to suffer with Me until the fulfillment of My redemptive work. For as yet My redemptive work is not complete. You have heard it said that the Lord tarries for the gathering of the last member into His Body, and then shall come the Rapture of the Church; but I say unto you, the Lord tarries not so much for the completion of a special NUMBER of people, but for a special WORK to be done in a people whom He has ALREADY chosen and redeemed! Yes, it is the PREPARATION work for which He tarries, and if you will set your hearts to allow Him to do His perfect work in you, you shall more quickly see the day of the coming of the Lord and will be prepared to have a part in the last ingathering before His appearing. The gathering of the harvest waits for REAPERS, and the reapers are few and feeble, for God's people are weak because of their selfishness and willfulness. . .because of much preoccupation with the cares of the world. . .because of fat and greedy hearts that do not care either for God nor for the lost.

Repent, else thy candle be removed; for Restoration must first come to the House of the Lord. He shall share nothing of My glory who refuses to be partaker of My suffering (2 Timothy 2:12).

GRACE IS MY SMILE *of* COMPASSION

Never presume upon My grace. I extend My grace to the helpless and needy, not to the willful and rebellious. The latter need My forgiveness. Grace is My smile of compassion upon the soul that desires to please Me but has not the strength to do so. In receiving My grace in such a state, the believer finds faith rising in his heart, and as faith increases, he is strengthened to do that which for him was impossible before.

So if you find yourself in defeat, seek My grace. With My grace will come My overcoming power. In coming to Me in this way, you eradicate discouragement. When you accept My extended grace, you remove your sense of failure. It is natural for you to reject yourself when you have failed. When you know that I do not reject you even in your worst state, faith will rise and slay despair. Hope will drive out discouragement, and My love will restore your joy.

You should never abandon your desire for holiness because of your failures. You judge yourself incurably sinful. I see you as potentially pure. When you can look upon your own soul with compassion, you will know that My spirit has worked a work of grace in your heart, and you shall be lifted above despair. You shall have a song of praise on your lips and a shout of victory in your heart. *"Sin shall not have dominion over you: for ye are not under the law, but under grace"* (Romans 6:14).

CHEERFULNESS BRINGS SUNSHINE

Cheerfulness brings sunshine to the soul and drives away the shadows of anxiety. To be cheerful under all circumstances is to radiate faith. It is an expression of hope and an attitude of joyful expectancy. . .it is to know that God holds all things in His control and that He neither slumbers nor sleeps.

THE FEAR of GOD

"The secret of the LORD is with them that fear him" (Psalm 25:14).

Yes, My child, if you would search Me out, learn what it is to know the fear of God. Make of your heart a citadel of sacred worship, knowing that as you kneel at the altar of consecration, you shall receive of My grace and mercy and you shall behold mysteries. . .things hidden from the carnal eye and withheld from the self-absorbed. For love of self will keep you from this place as surely as baser sins. You may shun wickedness in its commonly recognized forms and yet search for Me in vain if you do not lay aside self-interest and renounce self-love.

Heart-purity is like the wall around a garden. It will protect the soul against the invasion of alien forces.

I AM YOUR STRONG TOWER

You are ever in danger of walking in your own will when you give thought to your safety. I, the Lord, am your strong tower, and I would be your abiding place. He who hides in Me shall not be found by his enemies. Yea, though his enemies be the fears of his own heart, he shall find deliverance from these when he learns to abide in Me.

In My presence all fears are dissolved. Loneliness is banished by My fellowship. Darkness is dispelled by My light. Guilt is removed by My forgiveness.

Come to Me with your love. In the quiet of worship I will relieve you of anxiety and fill you with joy. I will lift the burden, and you shall go free.

DELIVERANCE HAS COME

"And when they began to sing and to praise, the LORD set ambushments. . .against [their enemies]" (2 Chronicles 20:22).

Yes, and I have set ambushments against YOUR enemies, and I will smite him that causes you to dwell in fear. I will not suffer your foot to be moved but will cause you to walk in the way I have designed for you and no man shall hinder. For I have set My battle in array, and I the Lord your God will fight for you and you shall hold your peace.

You shall rejoice and sing, yes, you can dance for joy, for your deliverance has already come, and the day of your visitation is HERE!

Lay hold upon the fullness of your inheritance for it is not for some future time, but the time is NOW. Be not dismayed by any adverse climate. Your peace is *within* you, and the adversary wars in vain. Be not dismayed, My child, and again I say to you, Be not dismayed.

Up! Arm yourselves with the Truth. Embrace it as your dearest friend. Let it not be displaced by worldly wisdom nor wrested by ignorance in such a way that it loses its power to convict of sin. For it is sin that hinders the flow of My power, and if you would move in power, you must move in heart purity. This I alone can give, for I create a clean heart in response to repentance and contrition. David knew this when he prayed, *"Create in me a clean heart, O God"* (Psalm 51:10).

Let this be your prayer and let My Word do its cleansing work in your hearts, for with righteousness comes strength, by My Spirit there shall be raised up overcomers and in that day you shall praise Me for the victory I shall bring to pass.

COURAGE

There are many places, My child, where only sheer courage will see you through. Prayer is the breath of the soul. Faith is paramount. Love is the essence of pure being. But none of these will suffice in the hour of stress if you have not courage.

Courage is that inner fortification of the disposition that is undaunted by the impossible, unthwarted by the improbable, and undismayed by the unthinkable. Courage makes perseverance attainable when encouragement is nowhere to be found. Courage is a stream of cool water to the soul when life is dry and parched. Courage gives stamina when love is gone, faith is wavering, and prayer is difficult.

Courage rises like the delivering angel out of the deep unshaken assurance of the immutability of the character and faithfulness of God. Courage knows that for the child of God there is no such thing as disaster. Courage keeps the destination in view and heeds not the intervening obstacles. Courage does not count the cost neither laments losses, because it reckons on unfailing supply and is content in knowing that one man's loss is another man's gain and rejoices as much in one as in the other—either to be the receiver or the giver. Thus it is fortified against the common complaints of man, for most complaints rise out of discontent with the role assigned to play. The genius of happiness is to reverse the game from receiving to giving, and in so doing, competition to excel becomes joyous—a soul-freeing expression.

Courage will compete to give. Self-concern will compete to receive. Happiness lies on the one side and misery on the other. Even prayer itself will bless the one and bind the other, for the self-centered prayer is spurious, and God cannot respond. The selfish man's prayer only thrusts him deeper into darkness and condemnation. The selfish man's faith is a farce, for it is misconceived and misdirected. His love is self-love, and so it is damning rather than redeeming.

And how does COURAGE effect the saving miracle? It is because it is the hinge which swings the door of desire OUTWARD instead of inward. It is self-denying, self-effacing, self-repudiating, self-sacrificing. Courage is the simplicity of knowing: God is working out *His purposes* through *every circumstance* of my life. His plan is GOOD, and how He chooses to act is none of my business, and whom He uses to bring it about is not my concern.

PATIENCE KNOWS NO DEMAND

Patience is the flower of love. As sunbeams bring a bud to full bloom, so love warming the human heart produces beauty of character in the soul.

The human heart is self-oriented and refuses to bide its time. It rebels against delay and demands to be satisfied. Only love has the power to silence the ego and temper the will. In so doing, it is working patience in the soul.

Patience knows no demand. Patience does not relate to and is not impulsed by self-will. Patience is content to be ignored and unrecognized, because it knows the purposes of God are majestic and unfathomable and move in a sphere untouched by petulance.

To cry out against the providence of God is as futile as a child protesting the motion of the planets across the sky. Prayer does not change God: Prayer changes *men*. The Word of God does not give man power with God, but brings man into a place where the Spirit of God may move with power upon his soul.

Spiritual growth is hindered by undisciplined zeal, for zeal is destructive if it is not yoked with patience. Do not fear to wait on God, for He is never late, and He never fails to manifest His grace. The mercy of God will move across the trusting heart as surely as the sun moves across the heavens. No hand can stay Him.

Impatience does not interfere with God, who is inviolable; it disturbs man's receptivity to divine visitation. The Spirit will not fall upon agitation, much as a bird avoids disturbance. Quietness attracts divine benediction, and quietness is prevented by impatience. Impatience resents God's silence and will not honor His wisdom and timing.

Waiting upon God is the most eloquent way to express devotion. It is to love God to the exclusion of all the demands of self and to joyfully give Him complete liberty to act in total freedom.

"My heart is resting, O my God,
I will give thanks and sing;
My heart is at the secret source
Of every precious thing."

ANNA L. WARING

Arm Yourselves *with the* Truth

Should I rebuke the blind and punish the deaf? But My people have been given sight and they have been given hearing. I shall rebuke them because having eyes, they do not see, and having ears, they do not hear. They have closed their eyes and they have shut their ears. They refuse to look, neither do they listen.

My Word is neglected and its covers are dusty. My people have lost their power because they have laid down their sword. They do not rise to battle because they have given themselves to pleasure and ease.

Will I be patient forever? No harvest shall come without the planting of the seed. The seed is not a smile or a song. The seed is My Word. It must be spoken; it must be read; it must be received and acted upon in order to bring forth fruit. Do not expect fruit any other way.

If My people neglect My Word, there shall be blight and drought in the time of harvest. Yes, and truly, the time of harvest is *now*, and the reapers faint for lack of strength.

HEIRS *of* HIS PROMISES

A merry heart and a happy countenance are the over-flow of My grace. He whose burden is lifted has much for which to rejoice. To be the possessor of true joy is to bring the atmosphere of heaven to earth. Mourning is for the desolate, and how can you be desolate when blest with My companionship? You are rich and ever increasing in all good things, for you are a child of the King and an heir of His promises.

Lift up your head, and let your gratitude find expression. True worship is the highest form of gratitude, and praise preserves the soul. He is ever clothed in victory whose garment is praise.

The Echo *of* God's Heartbeat

Persecution is nothing in My sight, My little one. It is a mere shadow falling across your path that is left behind as you walk on. It cannot block the way, and it is not a thing over which to stumble, for it has no substance.

To walk in the light is to baffle persecution; for the greater the light, the more the shadows are dispelled. Remember, I am the Light. You do not need to drive away the shadows. Abide in Me, and I Myself by the brightness of My presence will deal with the darkness.

There is nothing, in fact, that I do not conquer. I deal swiftly with every design of the devil aimed against you as you trust Me. It was because the Psalmist understood this that he said "The Lord is my *shield.*"

Live close to My heart; for he who dwells in the secret place and abides under the shadow of My wings rests in a place so secure that he is protected from the darts of the enemy. He is in a state of fusion where his spirit melts into My Spirit and finds a consolation imperturbable. It is a condition of infinite love and it transcends all conflict, even the tension between good and evil.

In coming to this place, there is an insight gained into the liberated life of the spirit that has broken out of the bondages of earthly experience and entered the heavenlies by passing through the death gate. Indeed, to come to this state of divine love and peace while still in the body denotes a death to self as real as the death of a body, and this death of the self life need not be postponed until the departure from the earthly existence. Indeed, if it is postponed, it makes for a weak entrance into the Life Beyond, much the same as a baby entering the world with a handicap.

You can choose for yourself a place as deep in God's heart as you wish to go. Relinquishment of your own self and love for God will take you there. You are there, I repeat, by FUSION with God's love: your heart and His heart melted together in Oneness.

It does not matter that you go alone with no witness that you have been there. Each goes alone. But on beyond, there is a jubilant gathering of those who have entered that state of holy ecstasy; for love is both at once very personal and intimate in its interior state and very all-encompassing in its outreach.

God is love. The soul that has experienced fusion can speak this truth as a testimony of discovery, not as a theological premise. He speaks it in conviction, and he speaks it in reverential awe. He speaks it in wonder. And he speaks it in a love that is the echo of God's heartbeat!

He Refreshes My Soul

The Lord is my Provider, I have no need. He lets me rest in pleasant places. He guides me in a life of contemplation. He refreshes my soul. He teaches me the way of holiness for His glory. Yes, and when sorrow and trouble overtake me, and my life is endangered, He is my comfort and my strength. He disciplines and instructs me in wisdom and patience. When surrounded by those who misunderstand and malign, He nourishes me with His love and kindness. . .He pours out His Spirit upon me: My joy abounds. Surely His mercy shall be my companion until I reach the end of my journey and enter the Father's house forever to abide in His presence.

(Psalm 23, paraphrased.)

VEILED *in* FLESH

Veiled in flesh, He hid His glory,
Christ, the Bright and Morning Star:
Stooped to earth, O wondrous story,
Left the gates of Heaven ajar.

Came to shed abroad His mercy,
Born to bear that holy Name—
Jesus, Son of God and Mary,
Came our ransomed souls to claim.

Blessed Saviour, Thee we worship:
Let our hearts Thy praises sing;
Joyfully we claim Thy Lordship
And we crown Thee King of Kings.

F J R

Other books by

FRANCES J. ROBERTS

COME AWAY
My BELOVED
ISBN 1-59310-022-1

ON THE HIGHROAD
of SURRENDER
ISBN 1-58660-730-8

PROGRESS *of*
ANOTHER PILGRIM
ISBN 1-59310-291-7

DIALOGUES *with* GOD
ISBN 1-59310-292-5

Available from Barbour Publishing,
wherever books are sold.